ROLLS-ROYCE

Jill C. Wheeler

ABDO
& Daughters

VISIT US AT
WWW.ABDOPUB.COM

Published by ABDO Publishing Company, 4940 Viking Drive, Suite 622, Edina, Minnesota 55435. Copyright ©2004 by Abdo Consulting Group, Inc. International copyrights reserved in all countries. No part of this book may be reproduced in any form without written permission from the publisher.

Printed in the United States.

Edited by: Alan Pierce
Contributing Editor: Katharine Thorbeck
Interior Production and Design: Terry Dunham Incorporated
Cover Design: Mighty Media
Photos: Corbis, Ron Kimball Photography

Library of Congress Cataloging-in-Publication Data

Wheeler, Jill C., 1964-
    Rolls Royce / Jill C. Wheeler.
        p. cm. -- (Ultimate Cars)
    Includes bibliographical references and index.
    ISBN 1-59197-582-4
    1. Rolls Royce automobile--History--Juvenile literature. I. Title. II. Series.

TL215.R6W49 2004
629.222'2--dc22
                                                        2003063644

Contents

Striving for Perfection

A journalist riding in a Rolls-Royce in 1908 called it the best car in the world. Many cars have come and gone since then. There have been faster cars than Rolls-Royces. There have been better-handling cars than Rolls-Royces. And there have been more comfortable cars than Rolls-Royces. Yet no brand has been as closely tied to perfection as Rolls-Royce.

Rolls-Royce cars have been favorites of the rich and famous for nearly 100 years. Kings and queens have owned them. Movie stars and rock stars have owned them. So have dictators and politicians.

One thing Rolls-Royce owners have in common is money. Perfection is expensive. The first 10-horsepower (hp) Rolls-Royce sold for about $800. Today the car is worth about half a million dollars. Prices for a 2004 Rolls-Royce Phantom with a 6.8-liter, 12-cylinder engine start at around $320,000.

The price tag is not surprising considering how Rolls-Royce cars are built. Major auto manufacturers can assemble a car in a few hours. It takes more than 800 hours to make the Rolls-Royce Phantom VI.

Rolls-Royce also takes pride in providing excellent customer service. Rolls-Royce fans like to tell the story of writer Rudyard Kipling. Kipling had a problem with his Rolls-Royce Phantom in 1932. He was at a hotel in southern France at the time. He angrily called the closest Rolls-Royce distributor. He asked that someone come out and fix the car.

The next day, Kipling told the hotel manager that he had not yet seen anyone looking at his car. The manager told him the Rolls-Royce service people had come the night before. They had fixed the car and left before dawn. The manager said the mechanics had not contacted Kipling because they did not want to wake him.

The Prince of Wales takes a ride in a Rolls-Royce car driven by Charles Stewart Rolls. Passengers in back are Sir Charles Gust and Lord Llangattock.

An English Car

England had few motor cars around the year 1900. Most of the cars in the country were made in France or Germany. Henry Royce was an Englishman who owned a two-cylinder French car. But Royce was an engineer and successful manufacturer of electrical equipment. He began to tinker with the French car. He ended up building three of his own cars, making them better than the French model.

In April 1904, he introduced his new car design to the public. The car was quiet and reliable and featured a 10 hp engine.

Royce entered his car in the Automobile Club Sideslip Trials that same month. It captured the attention of many car enthusiasts. After the trials, Royce was introduced to a young, wealthy car dealer named Charles Rolls. The rest is automotive history.

The Rolls-Royce Motor Car Company was started at the end of 1904. The company began building a range of car chassis. They ranged from the two-cylinder 10 hp engine to the six-cylinder 30 hp model. The coachbuilder Barker and Company completed the process by making bodies for the chassis.

Rolls-Royce quickly earned a reputation for quiet, reliable cars. The company's two-cylinder models could drive up to 38 miles per hour, (60.8 km/h) almost silently. That speed was unheard of at the time.

Charles Rolls took advantage of the company's speedy cars by racing them. He raced his company's Light 20 model from Monte Carlo in Monaco to London, England, in 1906. Rolls and the 20 hp Rolls-Royce beat the previous record by 90 seconds. It was an amazing feat since he had to wait three hours for a boat to cross the English Channel.

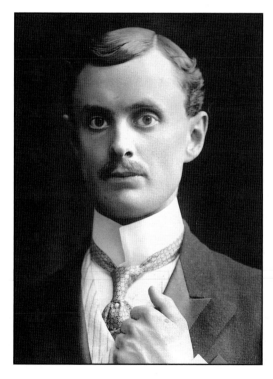

Charles Stewart Rolls helped give Rolls-Royce cars an aristocratic image.

Henry Royce was a superb engineer who designed the elegant Rolls-Royce cars.

The Silver Ghost

Royce designed a new car in 1906. It became so popular that it was the only model Rolls-Royce made for the next 15 years. The car was the 40/50 model. It used a six-cylinder, 7-liter engine. It had a top speed of 69 mph (110 km/h).

Rolls-Royce managing director Claude Johnson devised a way to promote the 40/50 model. He ordered Barker and Company to paint one of the first 40/50 cars silver. The 40/50 came to be known as the Silver Ghost. Half of the name—Silver—was in honor of the publicity car. The other half of the name—Ghost—came from the fact that the car ran almost silently. In fact, some people believed it was an electric car because it ran so quietly.

The original Silver Ghost completed many races and endurance runs. In 1907, Rolls and three other men drove it more than 14,300 miles (22,880 km) non-stop. This more than doubled the world record for a non-stop run. Rolls-Royce sold the car and then bought it back again in 1948. It is now in the Rolls-Royce showroom in England.

Rolls-Royce built 7,876 Silver Ghosts between 1907 and 1926. Of these, 1,703 were built in the United States. These rare cars were expensive to buy and maintain. However, they were reliable, silent, and well made. They were also easy to drive and made for a smooth ride.

Rolls-Royce only built the chassis for the Silver Ghost cars. Coachbuilders finished the car. Coachbuilders created many elegant, luxurious coach designs. Collectors prize these old Silver Ghosts today.

In contrast, the Ford Model T also was available from 1908 to 1927. However, Ford Motor Company built more than 15 million Model Ts. Model Ts were inexpensive and easily available. However, they were also noisy and unreliable. Drivers found them frustrating to drive and rough to ride in.

Henry Royce believed the Silver Ghost was the best car he ever made.

Fighting and Flying

Many Silver Ghosts were modified when World War I broke out in 1914. The fast, reliable cars made excellent ambulances, staff cars, and light-armored cars. In 1915, many British citizens heard the story of how a fleet of Rolls-Royce armored cars saved the crew of a British ship. North Africans had captured the crew of the ship *Tara*. They were holding them in the Sahara desert. The Duke of Westminster rescued the crew using a fleet of Rolls-Royce cars.

Another Rolls-Royce war story involves T.E. Lawrence. Lawrence was an Englishman better known as Lawrence of Arabia. Lawrence commanded a fleet of nine Silver Ghost armored cars in World War I. He believed they were the perfect fighting vehicles. He said a Rolls in the desert was worth more than rubies.

Lawrence used three Rolls-Royce vehicles to destroy two Turkish command posts. He also blew up two bridges, wrecked 600 miles (960 km) of railway line, and defeated a regiment of cavalry. He and the cars accomplished all of that in one day.

Henry Royce also went to work designing aircraft engines. He took his V-12 Eagle engine from the drawing board to testing in less than six months. In World War I, the British used more Rolls-Royce engines for their warplanes than any other engine.

Many famous people have owned a Rolls-Royce car. However, perhaps no one has experienced more risks with a Rolls-Royce than T.E. Lawrence. He used armored Rolls-Royce cars to fight Turkish soldiers in World War I. In World War I, Turkey and Germany fought against England. Lawrence worked with Arab fighters to attack Turkish forces in the Middle East. In 1918, Arab and English forces captured the city of Damascus in what is now Syria. Lawrence entered the city while riding in a Rolls-Royce car.

The Baby Rolls

World War I had weakened England. It had taken a toll on the Rolls-Royce company, too. The airplane engines Rolls-Royce had been building were no longer in demand after the war. Fewer people had the money to buy a Rolls-Royce car. The only car they could sell was the old Silver Ghost. Rolls-Royce management knew something had to be done.

In 1920, the Rolls-Royce Board of Directors asked Royce to design a new, smaller car. Chauffeurs had driven most Silver Ghosts. This new car would be designed to be driven by the car's owner. Royce went to work on the design. The result was the 20 hp six-cylinder car with a 3.1-liter engine. The 20 hp chassis was available for order in October 1922.

The 20 hp, or Baby Rolls, had just three gears. Many early drivers rarely changed gears, even on long trips. The 20 hp also featured a special grille. It had horizontal radiator shutters. Other models featured vertical radiator shutters.

Rolls-Royce built 2,940 20 hp chassis between 1922 and 1929. The 20 hp changed the company's one-model policy forever.

It became the basis for future smaller models. These include the 20/25, the 25/30, the Bentley MK VI, and the Silver Dawn.

   The 20/25 model appeared in 1929. It featured a larger, 4.2-liter engine. It could travel at 77 mph (123.2 km/h). That was 17 mph (27.2 km/h) faster than the 20 hp model. The next Baby Rolls was the 25/30. It was introduced in 1936. It featured an even larger 4.3-liter engine. It was replaced two years later by the Wraith. Rolls-Royce made fewer than 500 Wraiths before World War II ended production of the car.

Rolls-Royce opened a factory in Springfield, Massachusetts, in 1921. The factory remained in operation for ten years. Here is a 1928 Rolls-Royce car from Springfield.

The Phantom

By 1925, Rolls-Royce executives knew the Silver Ghost's days were numbered. The successor to the Silver Ghost was the Phantom, or Phantom I. It had essentially the same chassis as the Silver Ghost with a different engine. The six-cylinder engine featured push-rod overhead valves. The Phantom I could reach a top speed of 78 mph (124.8 km/h).

Rolls-Royce built just over 2,000 Phantoms during four years of production. They switched to the Phantom II in 1929. The Phantom II was the last car Henry Royce designed. He died in 1933. The Phantom II had a lower body and better performance than the Phantom I. The car could travel 92 mph (147.2 km/h) yet it had the same engine size as the original Phantom.

The Phantom III was the last model Rolls-Royce built before World War II. An incredibly expensive car, it featured a powerful V-12 engine and a four-speed transmission. Only 727 Phantom IIIs were built between 1936 and 1939. The United States was struggling through the Great Depression at this time. Few people could afford the car.

The Rolls-Royce Motor Car Company purchased the Bentley Motor Company in 1931. Bentley produced high-performance cars. Their vehicles had won the famed Le Mans 24-hour races in France four years in a row. The first Bentley to be produced under the Rolls-Royce name was a high-performance version of the 20/25. Later Bentleys were similar to Rolls-Royces.

The 1936 Rolls-Royce Phantom

Rolls-Royce in World War II

Rolls-Royce stopped building cars when World War II began in 1939. The company's focus shifted to aircraft engines as it had in World War I. Rolls-Royce engineers developed the Merlin aircraft engine in the 1930s. The Merlin became the power plant for Allied Spitfire, Hurricane, and Mustang fighter planes. It was the best aircraft engine England produced.

Rolls-Royce began making armored cars just before World War II. They were based on the Silver Ghost chassis. World War I Rolls-Royce armored cars featured quarter-inch (.635 cm) armor. In World War II, the armor was slightly thinner.

The armored cars had heavier wheels and mounted machine guns. Some had special tires for use in the desert. Special battle shutters limited driver visibility to a $1\frac{1}{2}$ x 9 inch (3.81 x 22.86 cm) slit. Just before the war, the cars were used most often for search and patrol missions. Some also provided support for army combat units.

A British Mosquito bomber flies over Canada during World War II. Mosquitoes were made in Canada. These bombers were powered by twin Rolls-Royce Merlin engines. Rolls-Royce made more than 160,000 Merlin engines.

The Silver Returns

World War II ended in 1945. Rolls-Royce factories in England had been heavily bombed in the war. That was because they were used to build aircraft engines. The company first had to rebuild its factories. Then it could resume building cars.

The company made another big decision at that time. It chose to build the entire car, not just the chassis. In 1939, Rolls-Royce had acquired the Park Ward coachbuilding company. In 1959, Rolls-Royce acquired the H.J. Mulliner coachbuilding company. Mulliner Park Ward remains a part of Rolls-Royce today.

The first post-war Rolls-Royce passenger cars arrived in 1946. They were actually Bentleys. The MK VI and R-types were in production between 1946 and 1955. The Rolls-Royce brand returned in 1946 with the Silver Wraith. It featured the same engine as the Bentley MK VI.

The Silver Dawn followed the Silver Wraith in 1949. It was also the first model to share a body design with the Bentley model. The only difference was the distinctive Rolls-Royce hand-crafted radiator. In 1955, the Silver Cloud I replaced the Silver Dawn. However, it had a completely new body design. Some models also had an automatic transmission.

The Silver Cloud II followed in 1959. It featured virtually the same body as the Silver Cloud I. The real difference was under the hood. The engine had been boosted to a powerful 6.2-liter V-8. A Silver Cloud III, and Silver Shadows I and II followed. These models featured small improvements and updated designs.

The Phantom returned in 1950 with the Phantom IV. It is the rarest Rolls-Royce ever made. The company built only 18 of these cars. They were sold only to royalty and heads of state. The Phantom V and VI were more widely produced. Production lasted from 1959 to 1991.

More recent Rolls-Royce models include the Silver Spirit, Silver Spur, and Silver Seraph.

Queen Elizabeth II received this Rolls-Royce Phantom VI in 1977. She was given the car to mark her twenty-fifth anniversary as queen of England.

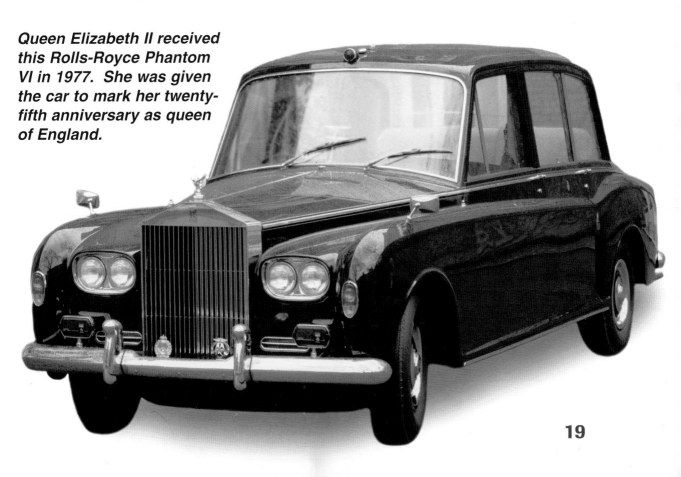

19

Hand-Crafting a Car

Most car companies make their cars using factories filled with assembly lines and automation. Rolls-Royce builds cars one at a time by hand. There are no conveyor belts or automation. Each car takes from three to six months to build. It takes one person a full day just to make the famous radiator. It takes an additional five hours to polish it. Welding and measuring also is done by hand.

Rolls-Royce employees take pride in using only the best materials. The wood in the cars is sanded by hand. Parts of the log from which the wood came from are cataloged and retained. That way the company has matching wood if the original ever needs repairs. Leather for the seats is ordered from northern Europe where there are fewer barbed-wire fences. The fences might lead to a blemish in the hide when the animals rub up against the barbed-wire.

The finishing process also is unusual. Rolls-Royces undergo a detailed painting process. There are layers of primers, fillers, and anti-rust treatments before the paint is applied. Coachlines also are hand-painted. Some of those lines are more than 15 feet (4.55 m) long.

The hood ornament for Rolls-Royce cars is called the Spirit of Ecstasy. Versions of the small statue have crowned the radiators of Rolls-Royce cars since 1911. Some people have believed the ornaments were made of solid silver, but that is untrue. The Spirit of Ecstasy is made of stainless steel.

Rolls-Royce engineers have done many special modifications to their cars over the years. They will do whatever a buyer requests. They have built cars that contained everything from pianos and bathrooms to refrigerators and roll-top desks. Rock-n-Roll legend John Lennon had a special rear seat in his Rolls-Royce. It reclined into a double bed.

Other unique touches show the Rolls-Royce dedication to high quality. In the newest Phantom, the hubcaps feature the linked-R Rolls-Royce logo. The logos are always upright, no matter what position the wheels are in. There are also umbrellas stowed in each door for the passengers' convenience. All models feature an ashtray that empties itself automatically.

Even the man who pioneered mass production of automobiles owned a Rolls-Royce. Henry Ford bought a Silver Ghost in 1924. He was amazed a year later when a team of Rolls-Royce engineers showed up at his house. They were there to do their annual service check on the car. Ford once said Royce was the only man who put heart into his cars.

Opposite page:
John Lennon shows off his colorful Rolls-Royce Phantom V in 1967. Some criticized the design. However, Rolls-Royce declined to comment on the style.

Rolls-Royce Today

Rolls-Royce has gone through many changes in the past 30 years. The company, which made both cars and jet engines, earned most of its money from the jet engine business. However, even the jet engine business ran into problems in the 1960s. The prestigious company went bankrupt in 1971.

In 1971, the British government took over Rolls-Royce. The car portion was then split off from the jet engine company. The newly independent car company was called Rolls-Royce Motor Cars Ltd.

Rolls-Royce Motor Cars still struggled financially. Vickers, a company that built military equipment, bought Rolls-Royce Motor Cars in 1980. Three years later, they lowered the price of some Rolls-Royce cars.

In 1998, Rolls-Royce introduced its first new car in 18 years. The Silver Seraph featured a new, updated design. That same year, both Volkswagen and BMW (Bavarian Motor Works) sought to buy Rolls-Royce from Vickers. A bidding war took place. In the end, Volkswagen acquired the Bentley brand. BMW bought rights to the Rolls-Royce brand in July of that year.

Rolls-Royce cars are known for their luxurious interiors. The interior of the Silver Seraph continued the tradition of using fine leather and woodwork.

Under BMW, work quickly began on a new model. It would usher in the next era in Rolls-Royce history. Project Rolls-Royce involved four years of design and engineering work. The result was unveiled in January 2003. The Phantom returned. It stayed true to the luxury and quality heritage of Rolls-Royce. However, it offered the best in modern engineering.

The all-new Rolls-Royce Phantom features a six-speed automatic transmission, a 6.8-liter V-12 engine, and a top speed of 150 mph (240 km/h). The car can do 0 to 60 mph (0-96 km/h) in 5.7 seconds. The Phantom is manufactured by hand in Goodwood, England.

Like prior models, the Phantom features a long wheelbase, short front overhang, and the famous grille and hood ornament. The hood ornament, the Spirit of Ecstasy, can be lowered out of sight when the car is parked. The interior features leather and cashmere.

The new Phantom is also the first car in the world to feature a special flat-tire system. It allows the car to run more than 100 miles (160 km) at 50 mph (80 km/h) even after a tire puncture. Once again, Rolls-Royce has gone the extra mile in its quest for perfection.

Rolls-Royce displayed the new Phantom in January 2003.
The cars will be built at a new factory in Goodwood,
England. A new Phantom costs about $333,000.

Timeline

1863
Henry Royce is born.

1877
Charles Rolls is born.

1903
Royce begins building cars.

1904
Rolls and Royce meet, and Rolls-Royce is born.

1907
Production begins on the 40/50 model. The car is later called the Silver Ghost.

1914
Rolls-Royce stops car production to build airplane engines for World War I.

1922
Rolls-Royce introduces the "Baby Rolls" 20 hp.

1925
The Phantom replaces the Silver Ghost.

1931
Rolls-Royce purchases Bentley Motor Company.

1939
Rolls-Royce stops car production to build the Merlin airplane engine for World War II.

1946

Rolls-Royce gets back into producing cars. This time they make both the chassis and the body.

1949

The Silver Dawn debuts.

1955

The Silver Cloud appears. It is the last six-cylinder Rolls-Royce. The Silver Cloud II and III feature a V8.

1965

Rolls-Royce introduces the Silver Shadow.

1971

Rolls-Royce goes bankrupt after problems with a jet engine contract.

The British government buys Rolls-Royce and splits the car and aviation businesses.

1980

Vickers buys Rolls-Royce Motor Cars; the Silver Spirit is launched, combining luxury and speed.

1998

Volkswagen and BMW enter bidding war to buy Rolls-Royce from Vickers. BMW buys rights to the Rolls-Royce name and Volkswagen buys Bentley.

2003

The Phantom returns in an all-new model.

Glossary

Allied: the nations that fought against Germany in World War II.

assembly line: an arrangement of machines and workers in a factory, where work passes from one person or machine to the next until it is complete.

automation: to operate automatically using mechanical or electronic devices.

bankrupt: if a company is bankrupt, it cannot pay its debts.

chassis: the frame and mechanical parts of a car, excluding the body.

coachbuilder: a company that designs and builds only the bodies of cars.

dictator: someone who has complete control of a country, often ruling it unjustly.

journalist: someone who collects information and writes articles for newspapers, magazines, television, or radio.

Internet Sites

www.abdopub.com

Would you like to learn more about the Rolls-Royce? Please visit **www.abdopub.com** to find up-to-date Web site links about the Rolls-Royce and other Ultimate Cars. These links are routinely monitored and updated to provide the most current information available.

Index